The Journey of a Trans

Vol.1

The Journey of a Trans

Vol.1

By

Ladytglitters

To all the people that made it possible.

I Dedicate

This Book to

You Nadheka.
THANK you for

Making me a Better

Person -
LoveYaSisters

Introduction

My name is Emma, I'm a girl who has a dream. But that comes after.

There are 26 years old, I came to the world in Riga, Latvia. Unfortunately, I have not known my biological parents, why? Only God knows! Perhaps one day I will find out!!

Grew up in England in a religious family. I came to live in France in 2012. We were in Paris at the time. Today I live in London. How did I get here? Good question! But if I told you any result, we lose the whole story!

That's how our story begins

Let me bring you back! While I was still a young boy

The family

As I said, I come from Riga in Latvia. I like to think my biological parents could not take care of me, so they preferred to leave me at the orphanage! Perhaps is it the truth or not. I personally don't want to know the real reason. At the age of my two years a man and a woman entered the orphanage.(From what they told me). My parents could not have children that's when they decided to adopt. Basically they wanted only one child; that's when they saw this little girl, very cute, but all blond with blue legs. (She had been placed by social services for adoption as her biological parents, were violent.)

On signing the papers for adoption. They saw a little boy who was crying because he wanted attention but no one would give him except this woman; it was then that from that days I had a family.

My mother often told me the story of arriving in France with us. The whole family from around the world was there to welcome us. We were officially adopted in 1998 by my mother in the French state. You will surely tell me that it is weird since I grew up in England, I will answer you: "I wonder if it is really to me that it is necessary to ask the question! ". The truth I do not know. (I know because it's marked on my birth certificate that's all).

It was then that we soon went to England. Me (Samuel), my sister (Diana) and my parents. We settled in a suburb of London, not in the centre. (And I personally understand them: the city centre is always crowded, it's hell to get around, especially if you have the misfortune of having a car.) In the Golders Green neighbourhood. I remember it like it was yesterday. Diana plays in the garden. My mother is in the kitchen and my father is in his books. To study religious education. As you could guess, we were in the Jewish Quarter of London. My father was well known in the community. My sister and I had to be blameless. I guess nobody expected what was going to happen a few years later.

I love my family very much, although to this day my sister does not speak to me any more because she thinks that I will surely end up in hell. Because in the Thora it is written blablabla ... That said , if she ever decides to come talk to me one day , she will always be welcome at home. Have I no family? how am I going to get out? These were the questions I asked myself just after coming out. But reassure you despite all his. I knew that my only way was to move forward. Is it true how to react to this kind of situation?

My Life in Religion

"Science without religion is lame, religion without science is blind."

- Albert Einstein (1879 1955)

In my family, religion is very important. My religion is Judaism. And my mother, my sister and my father are very religious they are called "haredi" is the term used for the Orthodox. Almost all my family is religious. Except me I believe in god of course. But why is it all fussy ? Is there the right to reject a child?

Is it normal to think that we will end up in hell?

Until the age of 10 years religion was the point of inking for me. I knew that no matter where I was! No matter what happens. God is watching over me.

But if he watches over me, why I did not feel in my place? I did not really know where to put myself.

My parents is my sister followed the instructions of the rabanims very seriously. All the rules had to be followed to the letter. Especially for the Sabbath. (Do not turn on the light. Do not wear anything on the way out.)

There was far too much prohibition for me. At that time, I went to the synagogue reluctantly because I had to make a good impression to the community being given that my father was a rabbi.

At some point I do not remember when it happened or how. But I remember not wanting anything any more. I completely stop practicing religion. No, because I did not have the faith any more. But more because I felt obliged to do it. I was going to be the damned son.

Theses day, life taught me not to see religion as something bad, but more like something that you can believe in your own way.

I explain myself. I believe in god, but I also believe in the fact that things happen for a reason but that we can reflect ourselves and not follow the laws of Judaism only because you have said it.

I have a stone around the neck that calls "the eye of the tiger" it is a stone that allows it's holder to be protect against bad spirit. And I as well do believe in the tenets. But I also believe of energy. Tenets are rules from the satanic movement, and I have found myself very impressed by it .

A Quick Passage to Adulthood

"Try to stay a child as long as you can. Do not force yourself into adulthood »

- Michael Jackson (1958 - 2009)

When I was only 9 years old. My school at the time was private.

One day, a teacher came to offer me a diploma. He said it was called "the gay diploma". A degree that will allow me to enter any University, knowing nothing. I decide to trust him. Because my parents taught me to trust adults.

At that time, I was only 10 years old. He wanted me to do things. I refused, and he force me we didn't have he same strength. And so it was that day when I had my first sexual relationship. (Blow job). I remember crying for several hours, because I wanted to evacuate what I had felt at that time. After what happened, I wiped my tears, and told myself it was over. But I was wrong.

After that, he came to see me every week. He calls his "the revisions of the diploma. "

A few months later, he told me that it was time to move on to the next step, I was petrified. That day, I had my second relationship. (Penetration).

I was in so much pain and crying begging him to stop. But impossible he was much too strong. I remember wiping my tears, getting dressed with my torn clothes.

I wanted to talk about it. But to who? An adult ?; Surely he could do things to me too, or think that I'm a liar., I felt so lonely. Every week, every time he came to see me. I disappear for a long time to be able to evacuate my feelings.

It had been almost two years since my first time, I still did not have a degree. That's when I talk about it to a friend.

He brought me directly to the director, and asked me to tell everything. All I wanted, was to know the date of graduation. Because I thought that all the boys of my age were passing this diploma. I was wrong. When I realised what was going on I felt so dirty, It was awful.

Once the director informs. The professor had been fired on the spot.

I did ask the headmaster to not say anything to my parent because I was really in sock and didn't want any drama at the time.

My father was well known in the community. You imagine the scandal! the rabbi's son is raped in a Jewish Orthodox school. No I could not risk that.

I just simply had to forget and never to talk about it, And life started again.

When I think about it today, I think my god! Why did I do that ? we must avoid this kind of thing. What is the best thing to do in these moments. I didn't knew what to say in those situation.

Despite the fact that , I know one day I will see him again. And between us , I really do not know how I will react.

Imagine the scene: I see him and he recognises me. Two choices are offered to me I play revenge or forgiveness.

But I know that I will play it, on forgiveness if he apologises for doing those things he did. I'm just going to tell him, "You've been doing this, and it has been affecting me for years. I had to take take drugs , pills against depression, but today I am stronger. Because I forgive you. I will never forget, but I forgive you. Today is another day, so stop thinking about it." I think reacting like his! Of course it's purely theoretical. We'll see the day it happens. Because the truth is, I do not feel absolutely ready for me to be seeing im anytime soon.

My Coming Out

"I've always said, I take my coffee as I take my men ... I do not drink coffee."

- Ellen DeGeneres

To arrive at the age of 13 years. The age of questioning. Despite what was happening to me, I really felt attracted by men. There was some kind of connection that I could not explain. It was like an irrepressible desire to feel the body of a man against silk. It was really something I was afraid of, and for obvious reasons. First I come from a very orthodox Jewish family . And second I only had sex once and it was a nightmare.

So I started to ask around some question , I did really want to know what was happening to me . And why do I feel more connected to boys and not girls .

At first I went to see a family friend, he was

a older than me and could perhaps give me a response. So when I asked he's response was. "How come you could think about about two boys loving each other? Never speak of it again ." But I really needed to know , what was wrong with me .

A few days later I went to see a rabbi to ask him want the religion say about the fact a boy can love a other boy . He's response was quite explicit. He literally said " homosexuality is a work of the devil . And if you have it you must go to a doctor or kill yourself ." I was really shocked about what he said , so I went to see a doctor like he said . But it was the community doctor which means he will not give the right answer. So that night I went to cry over a bridge and tried to jump, but then angel find me (I will explain, in the drag queen chapter) and explain me everything to me , on what it is to be gay; She did convince me that nothing was wrong with me .

So a few days later I decided to come out to

my parents . I remember that day, it was raining.

I was terrified of doing it, but I had to do it. It was for my own good. I walked towards them, and I said in a hesitant voice.

"Mom, dad. I like men, not friendly but lovingly." My mother set crying. My father was very upset, they sent me to my room and told me not to leave. For three days I was locked in my room. I had no visit except the governess who brought me food.

During the time that I was locked up in my room, I really thought I had done something wrong. Why can not I be gay? Where is the problem? I'm not asking a lot of things. I just want to be myself. I really felt very alone. Like a patient in quarantine. Like a beast that has been put in a cage so as not to harm the population. Or as a prisoner in prison. On the third day, my dad to ask me to pack my bag and to get on the car. We drove for several hours. During all the journey I was not allowed to speak; I saw in those eyes that he was disappointed, or it was just disgust to have a child like me.

When I think about it today and say to myself, that was the last time I saw him, it hurts me. As I write these lines, I mourn the death of my father because I have the feeling that he was not proud, and never was, to have a child like me. After my coming out my father and I never had a relationship father son. No real conversation maybe it is my fault, to have disappointed him . Am I the unworthy son that everyone thinks I am?

A Dream Castle Turning into a Nightmare

"The schizophrenic builds castles in the clouds. The psychotic lives there. The psychoanalyst touches the rents ".

- Jérôme Laurence

We arrived in a big castle with a big park. Everything was perfect. A kind of dream awaken!

And he told me, I was going to stay there for a while. It was only after his departure. That I needed to have a walk in the city before going in this castle. Despite my age, I was looking much older than I used to be , so I decided to go have a beer. Thinking that it will be probably the last one for a long time . As I was coming I saw the plaque on the castle. It was written "Orphanage- Correction House. "

I realised at that priced moment, I might

never see my parents again. I was abandoned again, I was alone. A few days after my arrival I had an appointment with the head of the educator, who told me that I was sick. "The disease of homosexuality", he said. And told me I was going to die. (For 4 years(all together)I thought I was going to die of this disease)

I wondered but what the heck. Do I do here? Postcard castle but behind her. It's hell on earth After my meeting with the chef, I was really worried about what was gonna happening to me . Because I knew form day one , I will have no support what so ever. Later that week, some boys from the center asked me to follow them. As I was very naïve I followed them , They took me into the forest, attach me to a tree and started to beat me up . I couldn't do anything. I was alone against them . For them it was just a game , (the game was to throw stones at me and the the first one to make me bleed ,win .) Once I'd bleed I thought it was over but I was wrong , (again) they left me there for several hours.

I could not talk to anyone about it, because I was gay, a mistake of nature, a sickness on legs.

I was always the person to blame in case of problems .I do not really remember how I managed to endure this suffering. I just remember trying to attend my injury the best I could, and I started to put foundation to hide my eyes swell.

Today I do not blame them at all, we all do bullshit when we are young. And I never spoke up about it.

Until today I have never talked about it , I do not even know if the perpetrators of these acts, will have problems or not. But it's not what I'm looking for, I just want to tell my story to help people who may be in the same situation. All that I can advise in these moments; it is to discuss it with a person of confidence. I know that it is something very difficult. But if we find the courage and the strength to do it, we could find a listening ear, that can be a help.

Don't be hard on yourself, it's not your fault, most of the time, they are just uneducated about the lgbtq+ community or they might do it on knowingly , in that case I need to report it to the police because In most of countries it illegal. And you can take them to court and have justice .

The Dark Periods

"Do not confuse the dark with the dark. The darkness aspects to the idea of happiness; the dark accepts the idea of greatness."

- Victor Hugo (1802 - 1885)

After 1 years of abuse, a new student had arrived , he had the same treatment as me. (He was gay too) . As I was there for the longest time, the responsibility of beating him up came to me , I had to hit him. I had no choices, if not it was me who would get beaten up .

I remember getting all my hate on him. In my head at that moment, I was happy to have discharged all this anger. All this frustration that I ever had in me, went in my punches. But at what cost ? the boy in front of me, was only 12 years old. After what I did , I was ashamed of myself, how could I get here? I couldn't even think normally after what I did!

That evening I made a suicide attempt, I was

feeling so bad and I preferred to be dead rather beat this young boy again;

Ironically, we found ourselves in the same room at the hospital. Him because he was unconscious,(I hit too hard). And I for a suicide attempt.

A few days laters When we left the hospital, I went to apologise, promising to never again put my hands on someone. I went to an anger management class to try find a way to take my feeling on something else, so I started to listen to music and believe or not it really helped me . Even today which ever I'm feeling , I have a song for it .

The group was so happy of what I did . But I wasn't . They asked me to beat the kid again ,I refused . So they started to beat me up over and over again . I was harassed almost every day it was Terrible, Over time I learned to control pain and roll with the punches.

Since that day I have never ever raise a hand on someone. For I know that I couldn't control that the day. I'm afraid that could happen again. And I know that if that day come, I might do something very wrong and regret it for the rest of my life. So I just prefer to roll with the punches and keep my calm because I knew that day what I was capable of and I don't want to see this person any time soon.

A Short Happiness

"All men think that happiness is at the top of the mountain so that it resides in the way-the climb."

- Confucius

A few months later, after all this was behind us , I had a conversation with the boy I had hit.

I ask him to tell me his story. How is it that he's here in this castle.

He told me, He had just turned 13 , he had been placed by social services. Asking him why he started crying. It was only after seeing a cane for the visually impaired that I understood.

After having come out to his angry father , And for punishing him, he threw white spirit into his eyes (it's a stain remover for clothing, I think). From that day he had become blind.

As I promised him to protect and take care of him. And as we were gay together, no one was going to help us. I decided to take the bull by it cones . I find him a school for the visually impaired. I bring him every morning and going taking him back at night; of course we needed to ask for help. With all the good intentions that we had , we couldn't do it alone .

We intend in permanent contact with the social worker who took care of our file and who help us both.

At one point we begin to have feelings towards each other. The famous boy I had beaten, who was unconscious at the hospital. had become my boyfriend. We loved each other very much no one knew we were together otherwise it was just be a problem.

It was then that we decided , with the help

of the social worker of course to move in together. Of course we were still sharpening the correction center, but as no one care about us , it was very easy to move out. We could have a cheap apartment, and maybe have a normal life . Without being worried or our security or else .

However to pay the apartment, one of us had to go work. Because he could not , I was the one going to work. That's when I found a jobs as a waiter alternating (it allowed me to work but also go to class.)

We where happy, I was our little happiness, only to ourselves. But unfortunately didn't last very long .

Death

"The mind forgets all suffering when sorrow has companions and friendship consoles it. "

-William Shakespeare

One fine summer day, I had a call from my mother telling me that my father had died and that I had to come immediately for burial.

I was the family man now and it was up to me to take care of them. I asked myself, "Who would do it? How will take care of my mother and sister ?" So I was like hearing a mission. You can not do anything without me .. you know this kind of things .

However, the family was still bored with me, because I think they saw me like the little black duck of the family , the one how does not belong with them . And after speaking to my mother . I could go to Jerusalem for the funeral of my father , but wasn't allowed to speak to anyone about my sexuality or whatever was happening in my life at the time . And nobody really spoke to me anyway, when we did meet my uncle (my father's brother) and my aunt. I had to pretend that all was well. I could not say anything. And why should I. I really felt very alone, as if I did not have my place in this family. That's why, back in France. I had to stay in the center, and keep working

I worked in markets and I as a waiter , I was 14 years old. I got up around four in the morning, went to work, in their eyes it was not enough. So I was working thirty five hours a week and dropped out of school, but no call. Radio silence.

I was devastated by the pains, the fact that my father was dead. I thought something awful like, maybe it's because of me that he's dead ? Maybe I'm not a good person. Maybe He was to worried about me and that's why he died?

I really did not know what to think during this moment; I remember crying for several hours. But despite this , I had to take on me and moving forward.

As today , Sometimes it still happens to think that I am a walking failure. That I will not arrive at anything in this world. Because I did not respect one of the paramount rules of law which is "respect your father and your mother".

I was gay. And for him it was the worst thing that could happen to his child, I hated myself during those moments. When I think about it, I question myself by asking myself.

Damn, where did I fucked up ?

Depression and Drugs

"One can find happiness even in the darkest places. Just remember to turn on the light. "

- Dumbledor, Harry Potter The prisoner of Azkaban

The moment the most disappointing of my life was to come. It was as all the joy had left my body; I cry for several days. It's crazy what that death can do, It changes us.

It puts us things in our head that we would not think in normal times. It devastated entire families; Of course we will all leave a certain day faster than others.

But I do not think that we may be preparing for this kind of thing. It's like a big hole that we have and probably never be filled again.

But that was worse than I imagine; I needed to slip away; To make sure not have this pain any more .

And that's when I started taking drugs.

This will provide me with moments of relaxation. Moments or I was physically there, but my mind was elsewhere. Just to allow me to stop suffering , only for a moment I wanted to forget all those things I have lived through.

But I lost control, I was drugged every day. I continue to go to work, I botched my work. I did not have anything in my head that I just wanted to go home and drug myself .

After a few months later , Kevin gave me an ultimatum saying to get me treated or so I lose him , and all we had built until then was gone .

And so for the sake of our relationship, I accepted to get treated. I was in the rehab centre. For my problem for almost 6 months. It was really hard to be there . But I need this it was for my own good. I did not get out of there. Because he thought I was too fragile.

At the end of the rehabilitation , I was still

weak when it comes to drugs. For all of the procedure, I had stayed in detox for almost two years . But I was at home going to work . I had to point in the centre once a week. And if he had any doubt about me taking drugs. They could ask me at any moment to take a blood test or a drug test. I really wanted to avoid that. As time passed I managed to do without drugs .

And my clean for a very long time .

As today. I would lie if I said, I am sober.

But do not judge me too fast. It was only after my arrival in Nancy and being fired from my job. That I started again . However, I manage to control. And I know when I have to stop not to fall back into my old demon. I could not bear a return to the centre. I am not so strong any more than before. I just have to live with it. But I make a lot of effort to stop .

But still I only do it socially , and just take a very very small amount .

My Walk into The Gay Community

"Being gay is not a Western invention. It is a human reality."

- Hillary Clinton

My way into the gay community was very surprising. I had meet just one other gay guys before Kevin. I knew that there were gay pride. But I did not know where to find very good places for gay night life . Kevin had heard that in Paris there was a gay district . So we decided to take a week end together in Paris for gay pride . We saw that it was a historic district too. As I'm a big fan of architecture and history. I was like a kid in Disney. It was so perfect .

After being tourists almost two hours we were quite tired . And we were in the gay area as well . We sat down at a very nice bar, (I don't really remember the name of the bar) as we ordered , I saw that they was a couple sitting next to us , so I presented myself to have a conversation with them. We learned a lot of things form them . They were much older than both of us. And we wanted to know how it was to live in a big city such as Paris ? How is it to be gay in Paris ? And is homophobia as bad as in the countryside?

They explained to us that living in a city like Paris was much better anyone that is gay. For we have not had to worry about what people think or say. It was much more open than provincial.

That being said they had to hide, From time to time , when they were in the street . He could steal him a kiss or two; but could not hold hands. To just do not have a problem. With some people in the street. Because although they lived in Paris, most of the french people are very racist and homophobic . It can really be dangerous some times , they just told us to be very careful .

And thinking about that now . Nobody knew that I was a gay person. Except of the centre . And some people in my family. We are back home the next day after experiencing gay pride for the first time . It was so good and so flamboyant. I was so happy to see Angel again After such a long time, but I never asked this. .

She was a man , dressed in woman clothing, So she said "I'm drag-queen, darling" . I was so impressed I wanted her to teach me everything that is of being a drag queen.

Drag Queen

"We are born naked and the rest is drag"
-Rupaul

My experience as a drag queen started when I went to see a drag show. My drag mom name was Angel . I met her for the first time when I was 13 , I tried to commit suicide that night. Because I had no clue about what was happening to me . (My coming out chapter)

In order to bring joy to me . She bring me at her show . I was really confident about me after that, she had answered all the questions I had about being gay . After the show. I did go back to my parents place .

It's only after a few years , that we met back again in Paris. I was so happy to her again .
And I asked her to train me to be like her a drag queen. She told me the secret to being a

drag queen is to be yourself but exaggerating a lot more.

With her, I learned how To get dressed, talk and even my attitude. But also my talent. I told her that I had no talent. I couldn't do anything. She told me not to worry . She'll teach me everything I need to know. She taught me to do the tucking, which is a bit complicated when it's done for the first time.But after you get used to. I remember the day

I bought my first dress. I am looking forward to having a good time. I spent hours finding the right one .

Once dressed as a woman. I felt good as if I was reliving a second life . I could be someone else who was not afraid of anything.

Once on stage it was finally up to me to do the show. I was really stressed but after a while. I was ready to break the house down . I did even find a new hobby that I really love . I love to dance, I dance all the time. And on that stage ,I had become a bad-ass girl, a big bitch how can also as sweet as a lamb.

I could juggle between the two without problems. I loved putting on make-up, getting ready for a long time. And when I went on stage, I was confident, I felt strong. As if I could face any problem , coming my way.

In my head I was the best comedian/ dancer . It was magic even during my second gay pride. I was a a drag queen . And I had a reputation. People recognised me and took pictures with me. Throughout the day, I felt important. I was proud to wear the colours, for a better future for me and the world. I became an LGBT activist that day . Proud to be me , and that is the story of the drag Queen named Ladytglitters.

Surprised Wedding

"The husband who wants a happy marriage must learn to keep his mouth shut, and his check-book open"

- Groucho Max

At the age of 17, I was still working and sending money, it was 4 years since I started this routine . One day my uncle called me and told me that my mother had past away . (I could not go to the second funerals unfortunately); so there was no one left to look after my sister.

We both arrived at the age of 17. And in our family it's the age to get married. But my parents were dead, and they are the ones who have to choose a husband. So it come to the first man in the family who chooses for the children. We don't really have the choice. That is the rules .Being ill at the idea of marrying a woman. I told him, I Do not want to get married with a woman . He said, "You do not want to marry a woman it's fine for me. I do not care how you marry." Then I told him that I had a boyfriend and we both agreed on getting married together , that way you will need to find someone for me as I already have one . He told me that I'm allowed to choose the gender but not the person we gonna marry.

I know a family with the same problem you will marry him. "(A gay child);

I was devastated not being allowed to get marry with someone I love . But I couldn't do anything . I cried a lot but nothing was changing his mind . I had to resigned myself to marry someone else and we broke up.

After a few weeks , I was asked to come and meet my future husband but nothing turned , like I thought.

When I arrived only a few people was there . And the meeting was where people usually get married. And in a blink of an eye I was married with a guy I just met .

Within a A few month I had lost my mother and got married. My husband and I moved to Calais (northern France). We had a large house. But at first everything ok but we didn't like each other at all , so he took the first floor with his boyfriend, and I alone in the second floor . I thought to myself here you are again alone . When it all started to get worse . He had forbidden me to leave the house, and if I tried he would beat me. When he had trouble with his boyfriend. It was I who was beaten. I was again harassed all the time , I was again the person to blame all the time . But it wasn't the first time that this situation happened , so I knew how to deal with it . As I promised myself I never hit someone again never so I just copped with it . I held 2 years in this situation. But after that time I met someone , Who had to be near my age. He was home hairdresser. This is what brings us to our next chapter.

Tommy to the rescue

"If you succeed tonight, more innocent shall live. Three rounds should be enough I think. "
        - **Harry Potter and the Prisoner of Azkaban, Dumbledore.**

Tommy is a young gay man. We first met at a common friend in Calais. At that time we were really close. He was crazy as me.When we came across in the street that we exchange our phone numbers. By promising to meet again to make a party pretty quickly.

A few days later the party was set . And he told me to stay the night at his place knowing that the next day , he will be doing my hair. However. My husband, whom I thought was gone and who was not supposed to be back until three days later, had come back sooner. And since he did not see me coming back. That evening . He started harassing me to find out where I was with whom. He was furious. I went back on the sly. Knowing he was going to take my phone as usual to cut me off from the world. I had the idea of hiding it.

Because I knew that I needed it case of emergency, I knew I was going to get beat up .

After the argument, (surprisingly to tired to beat me up) He went out to go shopping. And I knew at that moment that I would have no other chance to leave or probably stay and get killed.

I had to make a decision very quick . I did not think very long , I took a simple suitcase my phone is I leave the house. And I promised myself I would not come back. I was still alone. In the street . With a simple suitcase almost empty. I called Tommy by explaining the situation to him; the first thing he said was "come to my house right away, we'll find a solution. "

Because he too had to go to visit his brother in the south of France. It was then that he suggested that I stay some day at his father's house.

I could not say no; he was ready to help me. However, he asked me to keep an eye on his father because he had a slight problem with alcohol. I promised that I was going to try to do something sadly I thought at that time that it was a lost cause.

On his return we lived in harmony both. I remember we were doing a lot of vines (small video of a minute to make a joke). He introduced me to three friends of his. Laura, Sonia and Marion

Laura was a mother living near my ex-husband's house. She had a daughter who was at the time almost born (a few months apart).

she had two dog is a cat. (Zeus, Cyane and the other I do not remember any more.))

She was a a great girl a good living. And a very pretty smile. Often went at her place when Tommy was traveling. For at least change my idea and to keep her company.

I remember one day Tommy and me day staying at Laura house, to wake us up, we had play guitar hero. She rolled us almost every time.

This was very funny. Looking back I miss her a lot. But I think this is a can my fault because I'm not the kind of person to send message all the time but if you need me I'm always there to help if needed.

Sonia. Was also a wonderful girl. Always smiling . Very often going around the city in her beautiful Audi. . I went to her home often. To have a good time just chilling . At that time she had some concern for the heart (boyfriend problems) . Which I hope to settle since. She often gave me clothes she did not wear any more. I have kept every pair of shoes since .

Marion ,All I remember is what she works for Nu Skin (it's a cosmetics brand.) I do not remember much about her unfortunately.

One day Tommy met a man, (if I remember it was on the internet but I'm not sure) who was called Larry. Larry is a father of 4 children (if my memory is good). He holds a food shop in the north of France. (I do not want to reveal the location of the place) introverted but very kind.

Despite their age. It can be seen that he has experience. He started to see each other. And then, little by little, he went to live with Larry. Leaving me the apartment. However he was coming back the weekend to be able to spend it with me. All these people really help me on a lot of things.

Tommy helped me ask for a divorce. Unfortunately its still not finished today. Because he came without a lawyer during non-conciliation, which means that he had to wait two years before another appeal.

I remember one day or Tommy and me were walking around town when suddenly; we come face to face with my ex husband. We went back to a bank and he followed us. And did not hesitated to attack me in front of everyone. He even left with my cell phone to cut me off again.

Arriving at the hospital to see if I had anything that was broken I fall back on him. I had to ask the nurses to put him in a separate room. So that I can leave the hospital without him knowing #fml.

At the police station, it was magical. He said that , it was I who was to blame because I was jumping over him and attacked.

The police didn't even care about anything . This is France, when you get assaulted by your ex husband and the police just says that it's not their problems.

That's why as today I don't live in France . I hate France . To much things going on .

Trans-Identity

My whole life I've searched my body for scars Because I know a part of me is missing.
- From the film 'About ray'

After this all story . I decided it was time for a change that where nobody was going to dictate my life.

I thought, I have to make a drastic change, and I put a little money on the side , but not much.

Of course I told my uncle, who told me that , it was wrong that all those things happened to me. Since I wanted to change, the best way for me to do that , was to changing my identity completely.

I decided to change my identity because of my experience as a drag queen, I wanted to feel again this power that I had . I decided, that from this day , I will not show emotion. I had suffered too much. At that time I wanted to hide behind a character with a completely bad-ass personality. I could not continue like this . Today, it is true that my character is still in place. A carapace that nobody can reach. I do not want to suffer anymore. My character is part of me now, I am this character. And I may have lost myself a bit. I feel enormously better by being a woman , Emma who is not afraid of anything.She can handle any situation. Ready to help others and expect nothing in return. And of course a crazy little bitch.

I had a long discussion with a transgender girl who had explained me the process. Has my Appointment with the psychologist. I told him my story. And told me my change will take 5 years. I had waited too long, I wanted the change ,and as all the people that know me will say .I'm not very patient in life.

Again I needed to talk to my uncle about my

transition and told me he did not think it was the right decision to take. But I was determined .I had to do it for my own good. that's when I took all the money I had set aside for college and decide to go into the unknown.

It's really hard to think you're alone. For this big change. But unfortunately at this time. it was very difficult for me to find a listening ear.

But nothing can stop you if you are determined .

Believe me it's a very big decision , and if you think that can help you being how you really are . Don't listen to no one , just listen to your heart . He's knows what's best for you.

The Journey Begins

"Whoever travels knows that there is always a time when you have to leave."

- Paulo Coelho

My journey begins in Calais. After talking with the psychiatrist who told me that my surgery was going to take almost five years. (It means that in the days today I still would not operate.)

I remember telling him to give me another appointment one month later. Because I knew who I will found a way to make, the process go faster. Moreover, before the next appointment. She would have had no choice but to give me the hormones. And between us I have the particularity of always getting what I want.

So to come back to my story. My uncle gave me the advice so I needed it for my trip. But I must admit that I kind of lied to him. Because he thought I would go straight to Bangkok (Thailand) to get surgery.

But when I watch flights not very expensive. I'm falling on a pretty nice charter. So I had to fly to Paris with a stopover in Moscow and then take another plane to Thailand.

Except that I wanted to go to Jerusalem first .

I decided to make a small detour because I absolutely wanted to go to the grave of my parents it was for me the obligatory passage ,being given that I could not talk to them when they was alive I was going to talk to them when they are dead; and as I was sure they were going to listen to me . (well, you understand).

The weird thing about it is that when my father died, I cried for several days. While my mother's death nothing, I did not cry a single day . Is it because I did not love her ? Would you tell me. But no, I loved my parents more than anything in the world.

So why did not I manage to cry, what is it? .

I do not know. I can not even explain it to myself so who can. (I've often been told to go to a therapist to talk about this kind of thing, but it's so hard for me to trust someone I do not know.) Anyway...

So to go to the grave of my parents with the charter I had to fly to Paris for Moscow and then take another plane to Tel-Aviv.

Then to go to Thailand to fly from Tel-Aviv to Moscow is then another plane to Bangkok. To leave I had to fly to Thailand for Moscow is then another plane to Paris.

I did not hesitate a second to take the tickets. And here I am, part of a journey to the unknown.

Arrive on the airport of paris. I was really stressed. I did not really know what he was waiting for me on this trip.

A lot of question was in my head. I will really do it? Is it really a good idea? How will others react? Do I do it for myself or for others?

After being stressed, for most of the trip I arrived in Moscow. Being given the next plane to take was four hours later. What would I do for four hours ? I decided to go to a small pub inside the airport. After sitting down is ordering a coffee. I saw the waiter very handsome young man. He must have my age. A Russian named Mitya. I chat with him during his break asking him if he was gay. To my disappointment he tells me no. But he had already tried with a man" for the effect" .

After his break. It was time for me to leave so he gave me his number on a napkin that was on a table. It was pretty cool. He wanted to know a little more about me and also that I send him photos of the course of all the places I will go to . After a brief goodbye, here I went again in the air for my next steps, TelAviv.

Arriving in Tel Aviv. A great emotion flowing my body. I could not explain it to myself, I did not even know why I was crying. After having taken the rental car. I left for my hotel near the beach in Tel Aviv. I needed rest especially because I knew that the next day I would go to the cemetery to see my parents. That night , it was impossible to sleep , I was still awake at three in the morning . So I got up and went to the beach.

I arrived near the beach and saw this gay bar. By entering this bar, I saw a handsome man. But I did not care at all, it was really not the time to flirt with a handsome man. I had to think about my adventure because I could still turn back if I wanted to. (I was in full questioning)

The next day I took the road for Jerusalem. At the entrance of Jerusalem there is a large cemetery called "Givat Shaul". It is the largest cemetery in Israel. After searching for my parents' grave for almost 20 minutes. I finally found them.

I said nothing, I did not speak. I'm just Standing noiselessly like a hurt little bird, By the death of his parents. And I did not know who to call , so I called Mitya. We spoke to each other in the cemetery by FaceTime. Because I needed emotional support.

After being almost 2 hours in the cemetery. I thought it was time for me to leave. And continue my journey.

Given that I was close to Jerusalem. I went to visit. Getting to the Kotel The Wailing Wall, also known as the Western Wall, HaKotel HaMa'aravi or the Kotel, is a retaining wall in the esplanade of the Jerusalem Temple, located in the Jewish quarter of Jerusalem's Old City. Of the century, during the completion of the construction of the Temple of Herod.

There are two roads to get there. Those for with the souk and the other for the car. You can climb by both sides. But a bit of sport to ride would do me the greatest good. Moreover, I knew very well deep inside myself that I was going down by the souk.

. I arrived at the door of the Old City of Jerusalem at "Sha'ar Yafo" (Jaffa Gate).

This door dates back thousands of years. And who resisted several invaders during the wars that hit Jerusalem. Was just really beautiful, a historical monument. I was ecstatic in front of so much beauty.

Arrive at the Kotel , at the top of the

mountain. Everyone had to pass the anti-metal system to prevent any risk of attack or other.

After passing the security system, I could finally advance in the holiest part of Jerusalem. There were so many people that it was almost impossible to walk, without jostling others.

I could feel the fervour through the prayers, of the rabbi who called the gents for "min'ha" (afternoon prayer). Joining them I knew directly that it was not for nothing that I was there.

I felt at that moment that I knew what I was doing. There was no longer any doubt. I felt inside of me through the prayers and the songs that my parent was finally proud of that would become is that he give me their approval.

I then walked to the Kotel to thank the Lord for helping me in that voice.

It is customary to thank you and ask the Lord by a small words in the walls. A lot of little message was there. In these moments we wonder if God will really read our supplication. Because there are so many people ,how will he know that it is for us;

The answer is simple God knows absolutely everything. It's a bit like Santa Claus for kids religion versions .Except that in this case . God is not at our service. He will make sure to do what we ask. But as we often say, "Help yourself, God will help you." This sentence all makes sense.

Starting from the Kotel. I could see on the other side Al-Aqsa Mosque or Al-Aksa which is the largest mosque in Jerusalem. It was built in the 7th century and is part, with the Dome of the Rock of a set of religious buildings built on the esplanade of the Mosques (Haram al-Sharif) which is the third holy place of Islam.

But it is also a jewellery level architecture. Unfortunately with the political worries it is forbidden to go to visit . As it is located on the Palestinian side. If one day the fight stops I would love to visit this marvellous architecture .

Given that I was in the old city of Jerusalem is that I am fascinated by architecture. I decide to go see the grave or would have been burying Jesus Christ is calling himself the "Holy Sepulchre". The Holy Sepulchre is, according to a Christian tradition, the tomb of Christ, that is to say the sepulchre where the body of Jesus of Nazareth was deposited on the night of his death on the Cross.

Going back to my car park in a garage not far from there. I obviously to go through the Souk. A place full of flavours from around the world. But also souvenir shops. Babouche. Cup . Candlestick. Bowl , All was there.

We could see people going up and down the

stairs leading up or down the mountain. There were also seated shopkeepers who watched the people passing, sipping tea while smoking Narkile (Shisha).

We could really feel welcome. And for a tourist it's just perfect. Then go through Sha'ar Yafo again, I arrive at Mamila street. it's a street with lots of restaurants. Full of clothing shop, but also art gallery with master painting. Is very pretty works.

I'm not really interested in shopping. I was in no hurry to call Mitya to tell her about my day. It was then that I left Jerusalem, the light heart and ready to face all the obstacles that will arrive in the future.

Back in Tel Aviv I recognised former friends, with whom I was at school in England. We spent the evening together. Because the next day I had to leave for Moscow and Mitya, and as well to take the next plane to Bangkok.

Back to Moscow. I left directly to register for the next flight. However the stopover was almost 14h ,so what to do for 14 hours in an airport. I took a room at the hotel inside the airport to rest and wait for the end of Mitya service.

At the end of his service Mitya and me had a coffee in the airport. We exchange some kisses. And went in the room. After having sex for several hours. We rested against each other, naked. We looked at each other in the eyes full of affection for each other. When I had to go for my flight. we kissed tenderly, promising to call each other.

I went to Bangkok, when I arrived I really did not know what to expect. I knew that the clinic was going to send a driver to pick me up and take me to my hotel. But I did not find it there was no trace of this person. Only after I realised he was waiting for me at the airport drop-off.

The first thing you notice when you leave the terminal of the airport, it's the heat. There is a very dry weather. And considering the density of the population. The air is breathable but for those who are not used to the big city. You have to be careful because there is a lot of pollution.

Once the driver drops me off at my hotel. The lady of the host asks me to pay a franchise of 500baths in case of damage that I would have done in the room. I must say that I was pretty upset about that . But after a quick reflection I looked how much was in euro. I felt really stupid because I thought 500 batts was worth a kind of 400 euro. But once I converted the money on an application on the phone . I realised that it was worth just 12 euros. So in the end I had a been angry for no reason .
Then I left for the clinic. I pay for the

operation and an hour later here I am on the operating table. The only thing I thought was "holy shit". I was scared, but I was confident I knew what I was doing.

And after 18 hours of operation. I wake up in a room alone. I was completely in the gas. But I was happy, I finally became someone else. A new person. I had become Emma.

I could not move much with the probe . And a terrible pain . It's like someone stepping on you. You maybe find it as painful as a pregnant woman about to give birth. I remember my first step after the operation. I was in bed for three days, I was in pain. Even the 10 mg of morphine he gave me in pills , which for me did no effect. I got up and they gave me a walker.

I am staying in this room for almost a week to learn how to walk, wash while having the probe and pain. The doctor thought to postpone my return trip because he thought I would not be able to walk for a few weeks. And I had 4 days left before leaving.

And I did not even visit the city yet. I had not seen anything from Thailand except this room in the clinic. I said to myself "It's time you move a little. Hurry to be able to walk well as you can go to visit the city at least, the time you have left.

That's when I got up. It must have been two o'clock in the morning (local time) and I'm practicing walking. No matter the way, no matter how long it will take I had to walk before noon the next day. Because I didn't want to stay in this room I could not stand it any more.

The next day I had to prove to the doctor that I was Apt to leave the clinic otherwise he would keep me. So he watched me walk hesitantly wondering if he let me out or not. And I walked, I pretended that everything was fine. And I paced myself to show that it was good, but in my head I said "do not fall, no matter what happens , do not fall . "

After this doctor allowed me to go out but only with my driver because I could walk. But I could not go far. Because I was quickly tired with the operation, the pain and the pills.

But I still visit a can I have not seen anything interesting. But I plan to go back one day to visit.

On my return to Moscow Mitya was waiting for me but my next plane was not even 20 minutes apart so the time to steal some kiss had come time to say goodbye. I am promised that one day I do not know when or how we will see each other again. And that day I would stay with him for three weeks.

At my return on Calais. People were waiting for me and was eager to know how was my trip.

Sometimes I rethink of Mitya from time to time. I love him so much . But I do not think he and I will stick to it. Why ? Even if he will tell you the opposite, I think he's gay.

I'm going back to the psychiatrist. Poor thing, she was shocked at what I did. I told her all the details and did not have the choice to give me the hormones.

Homosexual To Pansexual

Of course it's happening inside your head, Harry, but why
should not earth be real?
Harry Potter and the Deathly Hallows: Part 1, Dumbledore to Harry.

After my operation I was finally who I really wanted to be. I was back in Calais. And all was normal. I started asking myself a question because I wanted to know. Now that I was a girl I could try to see what it was like to sleep with a girl. I did not have the opportunity to sleep with a girl before arriving in Nancy.

But I really wanted to try. It's a bit like a child who has a new toy and who wants to try it. Me it was the same.

Of course . I had already slept with men since my operation, but nothing serious.

Some trans people think, that once the operation of sexual resignation perform. We get the status of woman who means that if you go out with a boy you become heterosexual. And for me it was just not possible to have the status of heterosexual . I've been through so many things. I was beaten because I was not straight.

So I could not think that I could become straight. This is why people ask me if I am a woman. I answer them I am trans post-op. The term woman is often used for heterosexual couples. (I explain myself: someone who asks if we are post-op or not. And when we say yes. They will necessarily say to you ",your woman now. And so if you go out with a guy you are an heterosexual couple.) So to avoid this .I say I am a trans who had surgery done.

In general, the question that always comes after is "So, if you had surgery? Do you have a dick or a pussy?" In general I answer very often by the following question.

"In both cases, do you want it in your mouth? "

Seriously what is this mania that people have to ask this kind of question , is like if I asked the position with their partner during the act. It's really something very personal. I even received messages from people who wanted me to send them pictures of my vagina and I quote "to see how it's done . A trans post op" (These people take me for a museum).

And when I explain to them, it's out of the question because I'm not that kind of girls. Who make nude photos, and who will appear on the networks inappropriately . They starts insulting me, because I refuse. Or I have had and also boys and girls who was trying to flirt with me to ask for photos stripping.

I always answer in the same way to her. I am a good family girl. I do not do this kind of thing because it could hurt me for my career and my parents learned to respect my body.

To return to my story. I thought to take in the tale that I was maybe bisexual. But no, because it does not bother me to go out with a gay, a trans, a lesbian, etc ... As long as the person likes me and I like him/her/they/ them . It's done ; I love everyone. No need to cheat.

So I am officially is openly a "woman" trans post op and openly pansexual.

Those who brings us following our story about how I arrived in Nancy.

My Arrival in Nancy

The man loves so much, when he fled the city, it is still to seek the crowd, lie to remake the city in the countryside

- Charles Baudelaire

My arrival in Nancy began when I was still in Calais. I was still living at Tommy's house and everything was going great.

One day I was talking to a girl on the networks. Of course I did not think what could change my life.

We often discussed, moreover almost every day. We began to feel feelings for each other. At that time it was difficult to see because she lived in the south of France at her aunt. She told me one day , that she had to go back to Nancy, because she had to go back to her parents' house. Talking about it to Tommy, he suggested that I ask her to come and spend the week with us to really see if things were such that we imagine them. Myriam accepted without hesitation. And told her parents what would be a passage through Calais to come see me. A few days later and after nine hours drive, she was finally there. Next to me , I really very happy. However I knew that at a given moment we are going to have a problem because being the sign of Aries , I tend to get upset pretty quickly (basically I have a character .) But with a chance . I thought ,that I did not have to worry because I let things happen. My second problem was (because of my experience), I have a lot of trouble opening to me regarding love. That's when she suggested I come live with her. Basically leave the city and start again elsewhere.

I remember one time or Tommy was back in the apartment with a friend of his. And who had seen that the curtains were pulling, to burn it on the windows. Myriam to be naked in the bed. And me trying to slip away to go in the shower. I was a bit embarrassed but in the end we had a good laugh after that.

After a week spent with me was really very well I was ready to go to the unknown (it's my adventure side. I would go to a place I do not know and redo my life). When I arrived in Nancy we went to her parents who lived in a small village not far from the city . It was a house with a garden very nicely decorated.

It was the house style where you feel right when you walk through the door. There was his mother, an exceptional woman who loved the detective series ,reading books. However his father was at work so I had to meet him later. Come dinner time, I met his father. He had been working all day and was very tired. according to what Myriam said to him . He told me he did not expect me to look like this . Because I think for him he thought a trans was very masculine. However when he saw me ,he had a relieving look from my very feminine appearance. Later in the evening his parents received Myriam's aunt, who lived on Liverdun a few miles from Nancy .

After making the presentation we discussed the whole evening of my future on Nancy. So I told them that my project was to build my business in the future. But that for the moment I was going to look for a job to be able to settle in an apartment.

It was then that the following days I started looking for a job, unfortunately because of my masculine identity no one wanted to take me.

Come Christmas time. I was apprehensive because it was my first Christmas. I do not celebrate it before because it was forbidden. (because of religion); That's why the Christmas period for the first time made sense to me. I did not know at all how Christmas and the New Year would be. I let myself be carried by the wind. One of Myriam's cousins suggested that we both organise a banquet party for New Year's Eve. Because he worked in collective kitchen, and knew some recipes or even advantage to buy food by the kilo. Instead of taking them to the unit. After some meeting to discuss our role in the smooth running of the evening. We had agreed on the complete organisation of the evening. Despite the tight budget we had. We could buy all that we needed. It was only necessary to wait for the day.

Christmas Eve, We all got up at dawn. Because it was so much to prepare Christmas. After a brief meeting to share the spots. Myriam had to take care of going to various stores to pick up our order. His cousin was at work so not available to help us. And I helped in decoration. To arrive on the middle of day. Her cousin was still not there. So I started cooking. I started cutting, cooking, all our recipes.

In the early evening everything was finally ready. A sweet smell emanated from the kitchen, it was the turkey that was in the oven. It could be heard crackling in the oven and its juice flowing over Duchess apples making them melting and irresistibly good. The table beautifully decorate with a white tablecloth, a gilt table runner. Full of little stickers mark happy Christmas. There were also small gilding beads. And the cutlery was in little red sock. Everything was perfect. We were ready to receive them.

Some hours later guests finally arrive. There was Myriam's uncle and aunt, her sister (Sarah) and her children (Mim's and Alessa, (who was still in her belly)) as well as her little friends and her parents. Myriam and I were already in the house to help all prepare.

It was tonight where I met the parents of Myriam's little friend. At that time I find them blah! People not really extraordinary. I got an idea of them quickly enough. I did not know how to behave with them. Because he said something but think something else. In other words a fake. During the aperitif I discussed with them. But I could see that a trans had "their" Christmas table, he could not stand it.

However their son and I were the room to bring back in their family and we were both accepted into Myriam's family, and we got along very well. That's why I do not understand why today I do not understand his behaviour towards me. Anyway.

Arrive at dinner time. We were all seated I was doing the service and making sure everyone was fine for everyone. After the meal come soon the midnight hour, as well as the dessert time. It turns out that December 25th is also the birthday of Myriam's father. We had planned to surprise him with a simple cake that was sure to make a happy as it was his favorite cake.

And who says cakes says gift! Mim's had received a lot of presents. Full of play. I do not remember exactly the gifts of

everyone, but mine was a lovely gift. It was the two books that were missing from my collection. The books are named "Harry Potter and the Cursed Child", and "The Tales of the

Beedle the Bard" by J .K ROWLING written in English. I was really happy. I remember even starting to read it at the end of the evening. Mim's intriguing book written in English, she sits next to me and asked me to read aloud. I began to read until she fell asleep. it was a bit like in a movie.

After a good evening . we would rest because the dawn was not far.

Christmas morning we were all very tired. After the night we spent. I get up before everyone else this morning. Because I had to cook because strangely we were hungry. Given that we were five at the table no need to make a banquet like the previous evening. So I warm up the leftovers is cooking because there was not enough for everyone. So I made a simple turkey stuffed. Nothing very extraordinary. After having a nap is necessary;

Once waking up, Myriam was distant. I could see something bothering her. I did not know what. That's when I took her aside and asked her to tell me what was happening to her. That's when she told me hesitantly that she wanted to be a man. She had always felt like a man. I must confess that at the moment I was a little irritated, not because she confessed to me that she was trans but more than she had waited almost four months before telling me. That's why I felt a little betrayed on the moment.

But after thinking for a few minutes, I understood because she did not know how to announce this to her parents, her sister and even me. I ask her what name she had chosen. Because the first phase of the transition is the first name, it is a way to accept the world's gaze is to assume.

It was then that Myriam had become Issac. It was now just necessary to announce it to his parents. And the truth I did not really give him the choice because I knew it was hard for him. And I did not want him to live what I've been throw alone .

That's why I asked for a surprise meeting with his family. He was blocked and could not express himself so I took the front by anonymous in his place. His parents all simply said that he will support him regardless of his life choices. (I would love to have my parents tell me that) and it is from this day that he became Issac in the eyes of all.

New job, New life

Choose a job you love and you will not have to work a single day of your life.

- Confucius

After the end of the year holidays it was so much to find a job. After several searches that ended in nothing.

I've been introduced to a retired man who used to work at the town hall and who helps young people like me find a job. After several failures, I had a job interview at pole jobs to work in a restaurant in Nancy.

Arriving at the pole job , I introduced myself sat down waiting for my turn for my interview. The interview went very well but the recruiters was a little shocked at my extravagant odds. And told me he would call me back later. Leaving pole job recruiters would ask me if I was still registered for pole job because they had no information about me. When I asked the secretary she told me that I had been struck off the same morning because I did not came to one of the appointments. It was then that the anger got the upper hand and I made a scene because at no time did I receive any kind of e-mail regarding a meeting. In doing so I think the recruiters were even more shocking because I really wanted to work after re-registering and giving the papers missing. I was leaving while waiting for the famous call. After a week of waiting a manager Slajana (a 25-year-old Serb),

called me telling me that I was received for the training period. I was very happy .

I was finally going to work after so much time looking for work.

There was a week-long training to learn the preparation of the burgers and a preparation for the opening of the restaurant. The first day of training was to meet the staff members. As well as our trainers.

It was nice . We all became acquainted once we took our post. I was then a waitress.

A week later it was time for the opening to the public our manager was more stressful than all the rest, staff.

The moment came everyone was ready to receive, our first customers. Our take the orders . I even remember the quote we are often told: reactivity, smile and positive attitude. (The weird thing about this quote is, I'm applying it in my everyday life)

And then that all together we start to work in joy and in a good mood of course . We had up and down during all the time that I work there. But all this goes terribly well. Until certain customers are allowed themselves comments very inappropriate and it did really hurt. However most of things that happen down there . I never said anything because I thought to solve the problem by myself. However, certain situation was that I asked the manager for help.

Transphobia

"Pink Day is a remarkable initiative that draws attention to bullying and discrimination"

-John Fraser, Ontario Member of Parliament

I started being a victim of transphobia when I arrived after arriving in Nancy. All started after my move to Essey. I did not know the neighbourhood very well yet the landlord said to me that there would be no problem. But I quickly realised that his word was not worth much.

Indeed, a few months after my arrival when I returned or went to work people looked at me strangely. As if he had contempt for me.

One day on the way home from work, I was surprised to see that someone had set my mailbox on fire. I had to remove the glass breakers that there was to clean. After reporting the incident the landlord simply told me to move because people could not understand why a trans had come into the neighbourhood.

Another time I could not go out of my house because the key was no longer turning in the door. so I forced the door and realised that someone had put glue in the lock..
I had to wait almost two hours before the locksmith came to change the lock and it was me who had to pay the repairs .

One night . I went home to change, my friends was waiting in the car . It was then that a stone the size of a billiard ball made a hole in the breeze. Fortunately no one was in the driver's seat otherwise he would have been hurt or worse .

But that does not only stay at home in my place of work I often received insults. Of course all the guests were not like that . But I do not know why most of the time the weird guest was for Slajana and me.

I remember one day when Slajana and I were working we had barely taken possession of our respective posts, it is then that a man arrives in the restaurant and asking for a burger that is not on the map (he thought he was at the MacDonald). We explained to him that we did not have this burger but that we could give him a burger that very the same . The gentleman was so drunk that he said insistently. "I want a cheeseburger. It was then that he became angry. And we threw away all the coins he had in his pocket. That's when Slajana put him out . We had to report the incident. We were advised to call the police; once arrive and handcuffed the individual. They asked if we wanted to further and maybe go to court . But we both refuse. And life has followed are at least for a while. until one day Saljana and I went to have coffee before taking the shift. Arriving near the restaurant three young people between twelve and sixteen years old, and without warning they insult me; "Dirty fagots !! He told me that with a big smile ,obviously my first reaction was. I turned around and I told him by looking him straight in the eyes. "Who are you to insult me? He began to be virulent towards me; Saljana saw that he had his hand in one of these pockets not knowing what he had . We decided to leave, because it could be a knife or some other kind of weapon. Arrive in front of the bar to have a coffee (the bar is just across the square and located right in front of the restaurant.) The incident was reported while we saw another manager out of the restaurant very nervous saying "are there where? He wanted to solve the problem, even if it had to come to hand. Unfortunately he was already far

My last experience that really shocked me when I still work on Steak 'n Shack. Everything was going well it was a Saturday if I remember well. A group of girls had come to the restaurant. By ordering he told me that he did not want me to take the order. Those that I can understand , not everyone can understand my condition. I did not pick up and ,I ask another colleague to take the order at my place. Once their dish is ready I bring them the order. And that's when the ketchup sauce is in sight everywhere. The girls at table had asked one of my colleague why, the restaurant had hired me since I did not know how to clean a table. Once again I didn't say anything . I really try to keep my calm all my evening after multiple remonstrance and insulting I told them: " you will need to calm down, because if you still pushing me to my limits . I will throw you out of the restaurant." Then she went to complain that there was a red hair in the fries.

Nobody in the restaurant has red hair. I took the chips went down the stairs threw them in the trash informed the shift manager of who came from this and took my post. After twenty minutes the girls came down asking where their fries were. The manager came to see me is my ask in front of the girls ,where was the french fries I just told him "oops, I purposely forgot !"

He asked me why and I told him that I do not serve people who insult me is disrespectful to me. I come to work not to being insulted And all went very quickly after that. And they said to my manager, "How can you keep this thing? It does not have to serve the customers , we could catch AIDS!" My manager was annoyed about them simply gave them a refund put them out the door and banned them from the restaurant.

Morality but if you are good with people , people will be good with you . Spread love not hate . And never mess up with a waitress because you cold wait a very very long time for your food .

But it's not the only time transphobia has appeared in the days of today I'm looking for a job. Unfortunately I have send hundreds of CVs across France but I never had a response . Because in general it always happens the same thing , I am asked to speak to the person of the CV . When I tell them that it is me either hang up or he tell me that they will call me back but never do it. always working since this day. And personally I think that it is very well these demonstration for the rights LGBTQ + but to be more present in the society it would be necessary to help them to find work because it is like its that one will be made accept. Thousands of LGBTQ + youth are homeless for various reasons and can not get by because they can not find work. And I think that if someone presents their project for being the new mayor or president I think that at the moment I will go to vote again.

I live in London now and it's the best decision I ever took .

My reaction to Disease

Life, which shares in temperance, courage, wisdom, or health, is more agreeable than that where intemperance, cowardice, madness, or disease are.

Plato

When I still working at the restaurant I did not know why but I had a lot of back pain so I thought these may be normal considering that; I work in a restaurant is that I lift heavy load.

But then once I thought it was over. It had resumed more painful this time at the level of my legs. This is sad me a lot , because at first I could work in heels and it does not bother me . I could do both service in heels. Unfortunately in today's day I can not even stay more than forty minutes in heel.

All started at the doctor I told him I had pain everywhere and he told me that it is a simple sciatica. Except that after several weeks of rehabilitation and physiotherapy nothing changed the pain was still there. When I went back to the doctor he asked me to do more push exams to really know who was going on . After a few stays in the hospital the review was not exactly what I expected after I had a possible sclerosis. When I discuss it with some friends, they suggest to go to another doctor to have another opinion on the question.

So back to hospital for further examination. I wondered how successful I was in not having those diagnosed.

I was just wondering where my life is going to be, from that moment on. I did not know what to think because the only person I know who has multiple sclerosis is thirty and have been locked in a wheelchair for five years so I was really scared.

Once the results fall, and the confirmation of

the disease. I really felt like not really knowing what to do with his .

In this kind of situation I have to question myself and to make a decision . Of course I inquire about the disease on the internet. And I must confess that at the moment I thought of jumping out the window. However, I am fighting and I will continue to work of course I must pay attention of my health. I do not lift heavy things or stay too long standing. I have to find a way to not be too tired while being true to myself. I started the treatment against the disease but after changing the treatment five times I wonder if it was really that diagnosis . Because I have more doubt than before. And I really do not know how to answer my question. You're going to tell me to go see on Facebook group this kind of thing; but I can not get to the idea of the disease yet the pain is there. I feel it almost all the time. I wonder what I'm going to do the day I'm in an wheelchair .I'm really scared of not being myself because of that.

Today I am still in pain , but I have good chance of ending up ok so lets hope everything will be fine .

An Unexpected Encounter

At each meeting, a new story is written. Here lies the most astonishing mystery of the human adventure.

Édouard Zarifian, *The strength to heal.*

Once upon a time, in a small town of Meurthe and Moselle (Nancy) a party that many people were waiting for (gay pride). Arriving at this party I saw my friends and people who knew me. it was then that my eyes fell on this girl. She had a trendy rock style . Half-long hair, the glassy look is his smile to knock down all the girls. As I approached her I asked her name. it was a name straight out of a fairy tale. She told me that her name was Amélia skinny young age (19 years) . When I looked at her I saw some resemblance to Justin Bieber so that's when I called her "the Justin Bieber girl".

I presented it to my friends, she made a

good impression immediately. I asked her if she had come with someone or this March LGBTQ + pride . She told me no, so I suggested that she join us and walk with us. Like her we could get to know each other better. And here we are all gone for the parade. There was music people dancing and laughing and we were both chatting to get to know each other. I discovered that we fly almost the same centre of interest. architecture and photography. We were both like kids who had just met. At the end of the gay pride. I asked her if she wanted to come to a friend's house with me. She said yes. And here we go for my friend's house.

Arriving downstairs I offer her a drink and tells me that she does not really drink. I told him . I'm not an alcoholic but that does not stop me from drinking a beer or two. In talking with them I asked them who they thought of her. And everyone told me that it had a false air of Justin Bieber that's when we started to call it "the Justin Bieber girl". after this evening we are staying in touch. And after a second date. We both talked about books. Those who then bring us on the subject "you should write a book" then I took the wonderful journey of writing this book. it is thanks to her that the book has begun. And I must admit that I can not wait to see her reaction the day she reads the book.

I like talking with her even if it is only for a few minutes I can finally rest and listen to her sweet voice. Still today we speak via email . And it make me smile all the time when I see her emails .

My Trips !

Travel is the best way to get lost and find yourself at the same time. ...

I love traveling . Unfortunately I could not travel because of financial reasons. But today I will tell you how I arrived in England.

It's been several months since I try to go to a different country to have a new life and change the monotony. So I posted a message on a Facebook group to find work in England. That's when I get a message on Facebook with a job offer to work in a "care home" in a small town in the English countryside.

After answering the questions on the "DBS application" and sending the files I received a positive response to my request, which meant that the job was for me. I was so happy after months and months of research in France and England. I could finally breathe because I had a job. I therefore plan the departure on June 1st.

Everything was perfect . Until I received the call that will change the course of things. The recruiter calls me in panic asking me if I can start earlier because they have no one to manage the patients in "palliative care". I automatically agreed to come sooner.

And the race against the clock was launched, we were the 09 May with a departure on May 14th. When I announced it to my friends that I left the opinions were shared but the majority were of great moral support. All I needed was to take care of my apartment in France, make it clean and correct for the inventory. Unfortunately I could not clean the whole because the time of goodbyes had arrived and I had to take the bus for my trip. So I left this horrible task to Slajana saying that I had made the biggest but it was too heavy for me so I leave it in the apartment. Before leaving, Slajana and I were invited to a friend's house. Of the sweet name of Aaron (I of course changed the name). His majestically decorated apartment from the Victorian era. He cooked us, it smelled so good. Legs of lambs accompanied by a bed of fries sprinkled with a sauce (which I remember more the name obviously), with between a salad. it was so good; And tasteful . And the wine was sublime. I was afraid of being late for the bus.

After picking up my suitcases from Issac 's sister (whom I thank for everything she did.) It was time for me to leave for my bus.

So imagine the picture, Slajana and me, were running in the rain, with two suitcases of 70kg. The dream of a life lol. So it was after tears and hugs that I left France to begin my trip to England.

My trip started with the Nancy-Paris bus. The driver and me where discussing a lot of things .During the trip we were talking about cars and he told me that he was a fan of a foreign country police car.

Arriving on Paris he helped me with the luggage that was much too heavy for me. After getting on my side waiting for my other bus to London. I could notice that there were a lot of people, more than usual. I think there was a match tonight at the Accord Hotel Arena in Paris. The air was heavy, almost unbreathable, it was really awful.

After waiting for almost two long hours I finally took the bus to London. Different than in the first bus people did not really talk to each other. Everyone was tired. I do not remember making a stop before Calais. Because I was sleeping surely. About four o'clock in the morning we arrived at Calais, and we presented ourselves to the English and French frontier police. The French policemen did not even look at our passports, they let everyone go. While at the English border ,things were different. There was a queue of at least two hours. We all had to take patient and wait.

When is the time to pass in my turn. I did not know how it was going to be. And in the end he just looked at my passport and let me pass. Once we waited for everyone to get on the bus, we made ready for big boats. We were almost all amazed by the boats.

I thought "here I am gone for a new adventure. France behind and England in front. For the duration of the crossing I wandered on the boat. Once outside on the upper decks, I had that kind of moment when you think you're alone on the boat. You know like in movies. It was very cool .

I was really tired and all I wanted was to go to the hotel and rest.

But to go to the hotel I took the taxi. I noticed that the driver was deliberately driving slowly to get the meter up. But I was so tired that I did not say anything any more. Check in at the hotel I asked if I could access my room even though it was barely ten in the morning. The receptionist tells me that this is possible but that I have to pay £ 20 more. I still discussed the price because it was marked nowhere that I had to pay extra if I wanted to access my room. He just wanted to make money thinking I was a cheap tourist but no. In the end he tells me it's OK for £ 10. I accept and go up to the room. After sleeping a few hours I decided to go out and visit the neighbourhood. Unfortunately there was not much to see. You had to go to the city centre for that. That's why I went to get food to return to the hotel. The next day I took another bus to Yeovil, Somerset. You must probably ask where it is. Well, it's near the Sea, a few hours from London.

Again I had to take two buses. The first to go to Bristol, the second to go to Yeovil. The trip to Bristol passed meaningless I was peacefully relaxed. Once in Bristol, I really did not know what to do because my other bus was an hour later. For that I took a sandwich and sat in the meanwhile. A few minutes later the staff made an announcement. "The bus for Yeovil had an accident so you have to wait for another driver to arrive within half an hour. But unfortunately after several hours everything was exactly the same. I was waiting for the bus. And after five hours (that means I waited five hours to take the second bus.)

I was very tired again by waiting. But I was finally on the bus. After a few hours we arrive at the central station and then I could meet my contact who worked at the retirement home. When I saw the retirement home from the outside it looked like a kind of psychiatric hospital for the mentally illness. The atmosphere was really weird as if something was wrong. I say nothing for the moment and wait to see. But after two weeks spending with them. I still watched the reviews leave on the

internet by Internet users. Most said that the institution did not follow company morals, or even patient safety issues? Medication, that kind of thing. But I could not say anything. After a few days I was concluded in the office and the manager told me that I had 24 hours to leave the property or they would call the police on me. When I asked why, they tell me that my behaviour was bad. While I respected everything to the letter. So I called my aunt and yes , even if I do not have too much contact with them , my aunt and uncle help me financially. Once I took the situation into account, she sent me some money for my return to London.

Since my return to London I decided to live there for a while, that's why I go to work every morning and for the moment I have a room in a hostel. Of course I am always looking for new adventures, so that's why I applied for a visa for Canada and if it is accepted I would like to go to Vancouver and start my business there.

But all this will be written in a few months in my next book. I thank you for reading it and wish you a good continuation. I hope you will read the next book ....

Printed in Great Britain
by Amazon